GREAT WESTERN
STEAM THROUGH THE YEARS

edited by

Tony Fairclough and Alan Wills

D. BRADFORD BARTON LIMITED

in the Great Western Steam series

Great Western Steam in Action
Great Western Steam through the years
Great Western Branch Line Steam
Great Western Main Line Steam
Great Western Steam Miscellany
Great Western Steam in the West Country
Great Western Steam on Shed
More Great Western Steam on Shed
Great Western Steam in Close-up
Great Western Steam at Swindon Works
Great Western Steam—Preserved
Great Western Steam south of the Severn
Great Western Steam in Cornwall
More Great Western Steam in Cornwall
Great Western Steam in Devon
More Great Western Steam in Devon
Great Western Steam off the beaten track
Great Western Steam in South Wales
More Great Western Steam in South Wales
Great Western Steam in the Midlands
Great Western Steam—Doubleheaded
More Great Western Steam—Doubleheaded
Great Western Steam in Wales and the Border Counties
More Great Western Steam in Wales and the Border Counties
Great Western Steam through the Cotswolds
Great Western Steam around Bristol

Frontispiece: Unnamed 69xx 'Hall' and an unidentified 'Castle' slog in tandem towards Dainton Tunnel with an up express on 21 September 1946. By that date the Great Western had not yet recovered from the ravages of the Second World War and the engines betray the years of wartime neglect. [Brian A. Butt]

ISBN 0 85153 286 1

printed in Great Britain by Thomson Litho Ltd, East Kilbride, Scotland
for the publisher

D. BRADFORD BARTON LTD · Trethellan House · Truro · Cornwall

introduction

The Great Western was never quite like other railways. Throughout most of the nineteenth century, its trains ran on Brunel's magnificent broad gauge tracks, while the whole railway seemed to have been built on a grand scale. Following the changeover to standard gauge in May 1892 the Company at last seemed to be settling down into a more mundane mould when, after the turn of the century, a series of locomotive prototypes emerged from 'The Factory' at Swindon which proved very different from anything else seen on British metals. Austere in appearance, with long tapered boilers surmounted by a milk-can of a safety-valve bonnet, the engines of Locomotive Superintendent George Jackson Churchward certainly looked different, and when their performance on the road came to be analysed, it was realised that there was something very special about these machines. Although there was nothing 'secret' about them, the true significance of the Churchward specialities was not generally appreciated until the mid-1920s, some years in fact after the great engineer had retired.

What then were these special features which made Churchward's engines supreme during the first twenty-odd years of the century? The boilers, rated at higher pressures than used previously (225 lbs. per sq. in. on the larger engines), were coned to assist the water circulation and steam production, and in later years were moderately superheated. The other major advance was in the design of the valve gear. Having studied the de Glehn compounds imported from France, Churchward developed the long-lap, long-travel piston valves which gave these engines the power, economy and freedom of running which made them stand head and shoulders above anything else of their era. The only other engines to match Churchward's advanced technology were Maunsell's 'N' Class 2-6-0s of 1917, but other designers were turning out cumbersome and sluggish machines for some years after Grouping. Once the true significance of Churchward's practices was fully understood, the other railways were able to catch up and eventually surpass Great Western achievements, but for many years Swindon led the way.

At the Grouping of 1923, the LMSR, LNER and Southern Railway were formed by the amalgamation of individually powerful companies and consequently for several years, the friction between the ex-members of the original railways hindered the process of the new Companies, especially in the development of locomotives. In contrast, the old Great Western, with the addition of several minor Welsh lines, became the centre of a Group in its own right and the development of the Company, including its locomotive policy, was able to continue, untroubled by any of the difficulties which so beset other British railways. Churchward's reign ended in 1922; C. B. Collett continued to produce engines in the same tradition until 1944 when F. W. Hawksworth succeeded to the CME's position; and throughout those years the locomotive development was logical and continuous.

The Great Western was a railway of contrasts. For example, its highly publicised express services were excellent, yet many of the cross-country and local services were liberally timed, often with long waiting periods scheduled at numerous stations. Fast goods services and milk trains hurried to and from the capital to the outposts of the system, while hundreds of heavy freights rumbled laboriously from one refuge siding to the next. Likewise the locomotive stock presented a contrasting picture until the end of the Great Western in 1947. There were the modern standard classes running alongside many of the older Dean classes which dated from the last century. While it would not be possible to give full justice to the development of twentieth century Great Western steam power in one book, it is hoped that this volume, the first of a short series, will provide the reader with a selection of scenes which present a general picture of Great Western steam over the period of its final fifty years.

At the turn of the century the Great Western Railway was still employing engines of Victorian aspect on its principal express turns. The Dean singles have long been regarded as among the most handsome of British locomotives, and the graceful lines of William Dean's 4-2-2 No.3046 *Lord of the Isles* are fully evident in this view at Westbourne Park shed on 3 May 1899. The engine was built at Swindon in 1895, a time when the 'single' was having its last fling in Britain. [L. T. George collection]

An example of Dean's later express engines: No.4135 *Pretoria,* one of the 30 'Atbara' Class 4-4-0s built in 1900-1. Although credited to Dean, the engine shows many signs of the influence of the rising star at Swindon – G. J. Churchward. The boiler, for example, is pure Churchward, with its Belpaire firebox and pronounced taper towards the smokebox. This photograph was taken at Swindon on 11 September 1927, by which date the boiler had been fitted with top-feed apparatus.
[H. C. Casserley]

One of Dean's most successful designs was his 0-6-0 goods, introduced in 1883. 260 single-framed and 20 double-framed examples were built, of which 54 survived until Nationalisation in 1948. Of simple and robust construction, they were splendid representatives of the British inside-cylinder 0-6-0 mixed traffic engine and were to be found throughout the GWR system. This scene is at the Railway's southern outpost, Weymouth, on 11 October 1931, and shows the very scanty protection which the small cab provided for the enginemen of No.2364. [H. C. Casserley]

The 'City' Class 4-4-0s of 1901 were renowned as high speed runners, the crowning achievement of the class being *City of Truro's* 102 m.p.h. in 1904. These engines, with their modern boiler and front-end design, could outpace the majority of their contemporaries from other lines, but following the influx of the larger standard types became outclassed themselves on the GWR and all had disappeared by 1931. No.3710 *City of Bath* is seen alongside an LNWR 4-4-0 at Chester. [L.T. George collection]

The great break-through came in February 1902 when Churchward's first 4-6-0, No.100, took the road. Originally nameless, with a parallel boiler, the engine received this tapered boiler in 1904, having in the meantime been named *William Dean* in recognition of the fine work of the previous Locomotive Superintendent. The works plate was removed from the splasher in 1906, which helps to place this view, taken near Bathford Halt, between 1904 and 1906. Although adorned with a brass safety-valve bonnet and copper-capped chimney, the austere outline of the new locomotive caused an outcry among locomotive connoisseurs at the time. [L. T. George collection]

To meet the increasing demands of the operating department for more powerful goods engines, Dean introduced his '26xx' 2-6-0s in 1900, and 81 of the class were constructed by 1907. Although the engines, invariably known as 'Aberdares', had Churchward boilers, the general concept was still of the nineteenth century. No.2602 is seen at Old Oak Common shed on 10 June 1922, and has probably worked up from South Wales with a load of locomotive coal. [L. T. George collection]

The famous works plate.
L. T. George collection]

Following No.100 (later No.2900) came No.98 (No.2998). The third engine No.171 (No.2971) *Albion* had the boiler pressed to 225 lbs. per sq. in., which was to become the standard for many subsequent classes. No.171 ran as a 4-4-2 for three years in order to obtain comparative data against the performance of the French Atlantics. The early examples of the '29xxs' had a lever reverse which can be seen on the right-hand side of the cab. Notching-up with the steam chests full was a strenuous task for the driver and the later screw reversers were much appreciated. [L. T. George collection]

Churchward took a great interest in the fine performance of the De Glehn compounds running on French railways, and three, Nos.102-4 were purchased from the French manufacturers at Belfort. No.103, seen here at Bath, arrived on the GWR in 1905 and received the name *President* in 1907. The compounds were excellent performers, but Churchward believed (rightly) that he could produce a four-cylinder simple which could match the achievements of the 'Frenchmen'. In later years the engine carried a Standard No.1 boiler and looked much more 'Great Western' as it worked with its sisters from Oxford shed. [L. T. George collection]

With their 6ft. 8½in. driving wheels and long-travel valve gear, the 'Counties' were designed as intermediate express engines in 1904. Until such lines were upgraded to take the heavier modern 4-6-0s, the 'Counties' were to be seen hauling the express trains on the Shrewsbury to Hereford and Bristol to Birmingham routes. Although fast runners, they were notorious rough riders and few drivers were willing to press them to their limit. It is of interest that 1906-built No.3814 (seen at Bristol Temple Meads) carried the incorrect name *County of Cheshire* for its first six months; forty years later, the error was almost perpetuated on No.1011 but the 4-6-0 was named correctly in November 1947.

[L. T. George collection]

The '2221' Class 4-4-2Ts were often referred to as the 'County Tanks' because there were many similarities between the two types. The tanks' boilers were smaller, but the machinery and wheels were in common. No.2223 is seen here at Bristol (Temple Meads), but the majority of the class was to be seen at work in the London area during their comparatively short lives prior to the final example being withdrawn in 1935. The semi-circular projections on the side tanks are the ducts of the two-way water pickup apparatus. [L. T. George collection]

No.97 (later 2800), one of the great prototypes of the twentieth century. The first of Churchward's heavy mineral 2-8-0s proved such a success that a further 83 engines were built in the years 1905-1919 while modernised examples continued to be constructed as late as 1942. Although designed for the heavy South Wales coal traffic, these superb engines were to be seen hard at work throughout the GWR system.

[L. T. George collection]

The '43xx' 2-6-0s were unusual in that they were a tender development of a successful tank design. No.4301 appeared in 1911 to meet the need for a powerful mixed-traffic engine which could operate on the majority of the Company's routes. It is believed that the idea for a Mogul sprang from a suggestion by Harry Holcroft, one of Churchward's assistants who had been studying American practice of the early twentieth century. No.4381, with copper cap and brasswork gleaming, stands at Southall shed on 29 May 1920. Unfortunately, as the years went by, these hard-working engines rarely appeared in such pristine condition. [L. T. George collection]

A hazy photograph of a truly great locomotive – No.40 *North Star* as she was built in 1906. The 4-4-2 wheel arrangement was provided in order to make comparisons with the French-built Atlantics. The boiler had already been road-tested on the two-cylinder 'Saints' and it was the cylinder arrangement which claimed attention on this machine, for Churchward had adapted the De Glehn system for use with this four-cylinder simple. Two sets of Walschaerts valve gear between the frames actuated the four valves by means of rocker arms. The highly polished machine stands at Paddington shortly after entering traffic. [L. T. George collection]

The engine reverted to the familiar 4-6-0 wheel arrangement in 1909, by which time thirty of the graceful 'Stars' were at work. The rather spartan Churchward cab provided little protection for the enginemen, while the handle of the screw reverser was placed at the very spot where it was convenient for the driver to stand, hence the traditional GW drivers' stance peering through the front spectacle. [L. T. George collection]

The 'Stars', the first batch of the four-cylinder 4-6-0s, came out in 1907 and were twenty years in advance of anything else on British metals. The high-pressure tapered boiler, long travel valves and De Glehn cylinder arrangement gave these engines a reserve of power which enabled them to perform with such distinction on the heavy express turns to the West Country in the years before the Great War. No.4006 *Red Star* is seen at work on a stopping passenger train at Ashley Hill Station, Bristol, in 1908. [L. T. George collection]

No.4002, seen at Exeter locomotive shed in 1910, bore the famous name *Evening Star,* which of course, was perpetuated on the last steam locomotive to be built for BR, No.92220. When the 'Stars' were introduced, some GWR directors made unfavourable comparisons between the cost of these complex 4-6-0s and similarly-sized machines of other railways. They were reputedly silenced by Churchward's brusque rejoinder of "Well, two of my engines could pull three of those bloody things backwards!", a boast which was not idly made. [L. T. George collection]

No.4017 *Knight of the Black Eagle* sweeps through St. Anne's Park, Bristol, in pre-1914 days. The German name was removed from the engine in August 1914 and replaced by the more acceptable *Knight of Liége.*

[L. T. George collection]

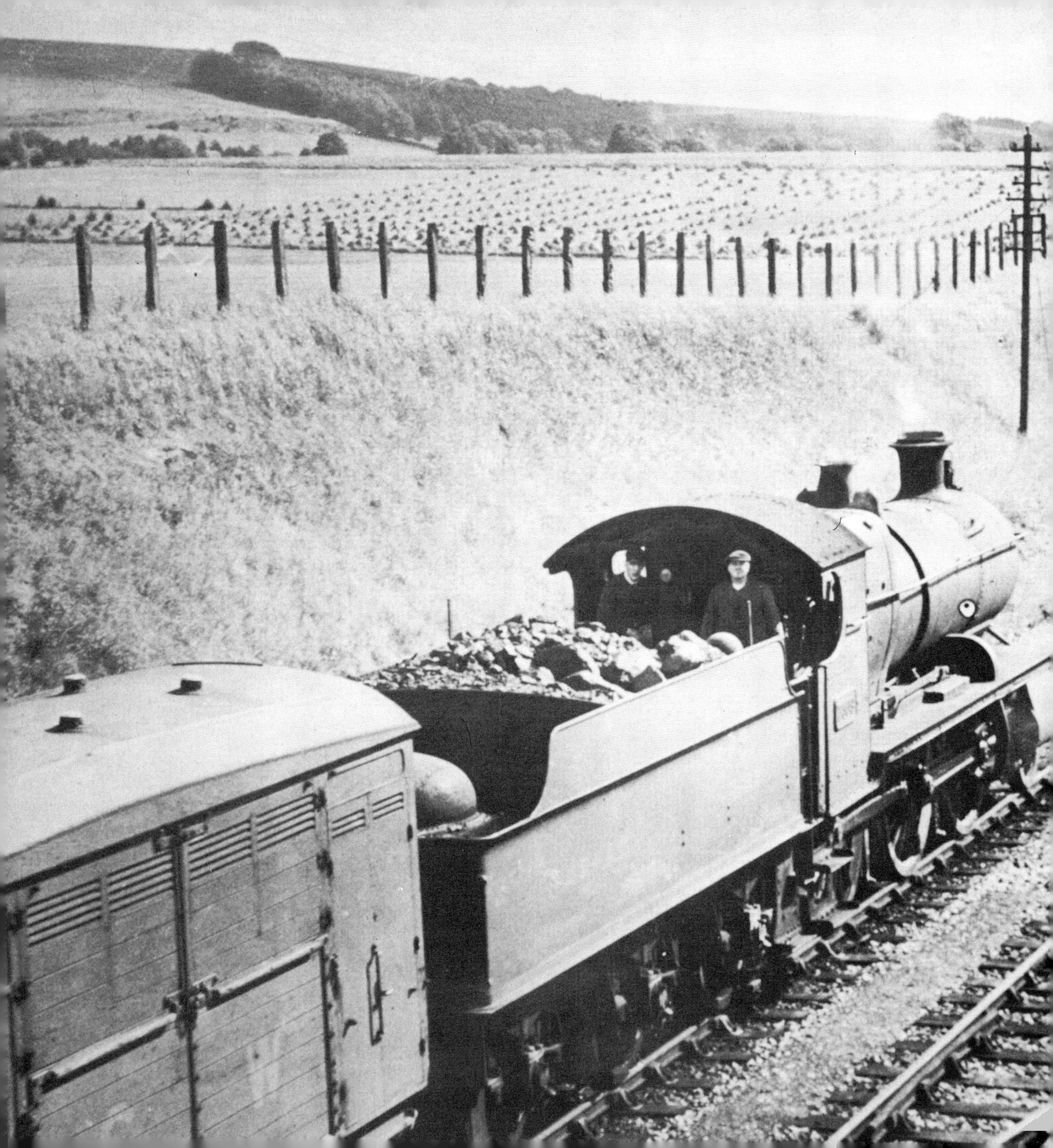

A Churchward Mogul runs southwards near Heytesbury with a Bristol to Portsmouth train on 14 September 1936. The large lumps of good quality Welsh steam coal will keep No.7309 bowling busily along towards Salisbury on this well-patronised service. Now, forty years later, the line is served by multiple-units, and the neatly proportioned haystacks and stooks of corn have gone the way of the steam engine, replaced on this rolling Wiltshire countryside by the ubiquitous combine harvester.
[H. C. Casserley]

Unlike the CMEs of many other railways, Churchward was responsible for the running, as well as the construction and heavy maintenance, of the Great Western locomotives. He initiated the modernisation of many of the locomotive depots, the first major task being the construction of the huge new shed at Old Oak Common which was completed in 1906. Four turntables were accommodated under the one roof, while extensive maintenance facilities were provided in the twelve-bay repair shop. This early view in the roundhouse shows No.2915 *St. Bartholomew* and No.3809 *County Wexford* on the right.

[L. T. George collection]

Churchward's solitary 4-6-2, No.111 *The Great Bear,* built in 1908, was the first Pacific to run on a British railway. The cylinders and motion of the 142ton-engine were identical to those of the 'Stars', but an enlarged boiler was provided, while the eight-wheeled bogie tender completed the *ensemble.* Unfortunately the Civil Engineer viewed the great machine with a jaundiced eye, and so she was confined to the Paddington to Bristol line. This pre-War view shows the engine on an express train at Bath.

[L. T. George collection]

The thirty-one members of Dean's '36xx' 2-4-2Ts performed local services around the capital in the early years of the century. Introduced in 1900, the final engine was withdrawn in 1934, following the introduction of the powerful '61xx' 2-6-2Ts. No.3600 is seen at Reading on 23 May 1925. [P. J. T. Reed]

Churchward rebuilt twenty Dean 0-6-0s into 2-6-2 tanks for passenger work. Little of the original engine above the frames remained, as a modern Churchward boiler pressed to 200 lb. per sq. in. provided the power. No.3908 was originally 0-6-0 No.2497. [Peter Winding collection]

Veteran Armstrong 0-6-0 'Standard Goods' No.1111, built in 1871, was photographed at Reading on 26 September 1925. Out of a total of 310 of these reliable engines built, 72 saw service after the Grouping in 1923. [P. J. T. Reed]

Another Victorian veteran, No.3505, at Wellington, (Shropshire) on 14 August 1926. The double-framed 2-4-0 'Stellas' were built in 1885 as broad gauge locomotives, and being comparatively new were converted in 1892 after the great 'change-over' of gauges. [P. J. T. Reed]

No.3593 was built as one of Dean's 140 2-4-0 'Metropolitan Tanks' but was converted to the 2-4-2T arrangement in 1905. The scene is Reading on 17 July 1926. [P. J. T. Reed]

Churchward introduced the powerful '42xx' 2-8-0 tanks in 1910 for use on heavy short-haul coal trains from the South Wales pits to the Bristol Channel ports. These were splendid machines in the true Churchward tradition of rugged power. No.5225, built in May 1924, was an exhibit at the Darlington Centenary celebrations in July 1925. [P. J. T. Reed]

No.3112 was the third of Churchward's large 2-6-2 passenger tanks to be built. The '31xxs' (later '51xxs') introduced in 1903, formed the basis of the large family of engines numbered in the 41, 51, and 61 series, which eventually came to monopolise the heavier local passenger turns on the Western. With 5ft. 8in. wheels and 200 lbs. per sq. in. boiler pressure, these engines were standard with the later Moguls, introduced in 1911. [L. T. George collection]

This view inside Old Oak Common in 1933 shows No.4702 on one of the four under-girder 65ft. turntables inside the shed. The nine '47xx' 2-8-0s were Churchward's final design to appear and with their 5ft. 8in. wheels were intended as heavy mixed traffic engines. They amply fulfilled their designer's expectations but were of rather resticted route availability and the later 'Halls' and 'Castles' were produced in large numbers in their stead. As much of their working lives were spent on heavy night freights they always wore a slight air of mystery which added to their fascination. [Peter Winding collection]

Most large depots had a steam crane available to cope with routine work, such as relaying, serious emergencies and derailments. Crane No.7, with its match truck, is seen inside Old Oak Common in the early years of the century. The men in the breakdown gang had to be prepared to drop everything and go when an emergency arose, and the rerailing of locomotives required considerable skill from the engineer in charge of the operation.
[L. T. George collection]

The prototype No.4700 on show at the Darlington Centenary Exhibition, 11 July 1925. [P. J. T. Reed]

The Great Western Railway did not suffer the traumatic upheaval at Grouping which most of the other major companies had to endure. However, numerous smaller Welsh companies were absorbed, along with their locomotive stock. Many of these engines were scrapped as soon as possible; others were rebuilt with standard GW boilers, while a few worked on for years in their original condition. No.908 (ex C.R. No.48) was one of ninety-nine engines absorbed from the Cambrian Railway. When seen at Oswestry on 25 September 1938, the engine had acquired a Western boiler and tender to match.

[L. T. George collection]

Twenty-nine locomotives were taken into stock from the small Midland & South Western Junction Railway. No.1126 (ex No.8) seen at Gloucester on 23 June 1935 was one of the six out of nine Tyrell 5ft. 9in. 4-4-0s which were rebuilt with Swindon boilers following Grouping. These locomotives continued to work on their old line from Cheltenham to Southampton until 1938 when the last of the class was withdrawn. [L. T. George collection]

No.1121 has full steam up at 160 lbs. per sq. in. as the 4-4-0 prepares to leave Swindon, *c.* 1930. [Peter Winding collection]

Fifteen small tanks, of which seven were named, came from the Burry Port & Gwendraeth Valley Railway. No.2197 *Pioneer,* weighing 36 tons, was built by Hudswell Clarke (No.871) in 1909 and remained in service until 1955. [Peter Winding]

The Alexandra Docks and Railway Company contributed 39 locomotives to the GW stock in 1923, the most modern being a pair of 65-ton 2-6-2 tanks built by Hawthorn Leslie in 1920. No.1206, seen at Newport Pill shed in June 1939, was a powerful engine, with its 23,210 lbs. of tractive effort and it continued to work until the 1950s.
[L. T. George collection]

0-6-2T No.277 was originally Barry Railway No.126 of Hosgood's 'B1' Class of 1890. Forty-two of these 55-ton engines were built for the busy Welsh line, which handed over 148 locomotives to the GWR. Although the engines from the Welsh constituent companies were usually maintained at Caerphilly or Barry, No.277 has put in an appearance at Swindon Works. [Peter Winding]

No.366 came from the largest of the Welsh constituent companies, the Taff Vale Railway, which had a stock of 275 locomotives at Grouping. Originally No.132, this 5ft. 3in. 0-6-2T of Cameron's 'A' Class has been 'Great Westernised' with a modern tapered boiler, and the 58 engines of the class, which were built between 1914 and 1921, remained hard at work on mixed-traffic turns in the mining valleys until 1953, when withdrawals began, the final engine going for scrap in 1958. The engine is taking water at Treherbert shed on 27 June 1938. [H. C. Casserley]

Overleaf: Handsome little 2-4-0 No.1336 stands inside the old roundhouse at Reading on 23 August 1930. Built by Dübs as M.S.W.J.R. No.12 in 1894, No.1336 and her two sisters (Nos.1334/5) were kept at work until the early 1950s, giving the enthusiast some variety amongst the large number of Great Western standard types. Outside the shed can be seen a 2-6-2 tank, a 'Star', an 'Aberdare', an R.O.D. 2-8-0 and a Churchward Mogul, a typical cross section of the many classes which were to be seen at Reading in 1930, at which date the shed was in the throes of modernisation. The roundhouse layout was changed into the straight-road shed which operated until 1965. [H. C. Casserley]

1336

Very small tank engines have always possessed a fascination of their own, perhaps because they make such a contrast with the largest main-line types. Also, they were often of individual design, as was No.824, pictured here inside Oswestry Works in May 1936. Built by Manning, Wardle in 1865, for the Mawddwy Railway, the 17-ton 0-6-0ST passed into Cambrian Railway ownership in 1911 and then was GW-owned until 1940 when it was scrapped. [L.T. George collection]

Another neat tank design, No.1338 was built as No.5 for the Cardiff Railway by Kitson (No.3799) in 1898. Weighing 25 tons, this little engine spent many of its Great Western years shunting at Bridgwater Docks, this photograph being on location on 8 December 1947. Sister engine No.1329 was withdrawn in 1934, but No.1338 soldiered on until 1963, when its work was handed over to a diesel shunter. Such was its popularity that it was rescued from oblivion and now is at the Somerset Railway Museum, Bleadon and Uphill station. [L. T. George collection]

The Great Western purchased 100 of the Robinson 2-8-0 heavy goods engines which were surplus to requirements after the Great War. These robust and straightforward machines had been built in large numbers for the Railway Operating Division and had proved their worth on war service in many parts of the world. Eventually the GWR retained fifty in service and they worked side by side with the standard Churchward '28xxs' until 1958, when the last example was withdrawn. As with the absorbed engines, GW features replaced some of the original components but No.3030, seen near Leamington Spa with a load of locomotive coal in 1928, still retains its graceful Robinson chimney. Below, No.3014 steams along the seashore near Dawlish. The R.O.Ds were strong, reliable engines, although no Western driver would ever admit that they were the equal of a '28'!

[L. T. George collection]

In order to provide modern motive power for the Welsh valley services Collett introduced the '56xx' 0-6-2 tanks in 1924. Two hundred examples were produced, the majority spending their working lives in the valleys. With 200 lbs. per sq. in. in the boilers, and 4ft 7½in. wheels, their tractive effort of 25,800 lbs. was put to full use on both freight and passenger work. Strangely enough, neither of these photographs show '56xx's' at work in Wales. No.5689 was a regular at Westbury for many years and was on shed on 21 October 1934. The engine, with two sisters, helped to bank heavy freights up the Salisbury line out of Westbury, as well as working pick-up goods turns. [L. T. George collection]

No.5619 was shunting at Paddington on 20 June 1925, shortly after its construction, having been sent new to Old Oak Common. [P. J. T. Reed]

No.4088 *Dartmouth Castle* at speed on the main line near Lavington with an express from the West of England on 23 September 1935. At that date Collett 4000-gallon tenders were standard for the class, but the engine is partnered to a Collett 3500-gallon tender, while the tall safety-valve bonnet looks most odd atop the 'Castle' boiler. [L. T. George collection]

A new era came to the GWR with the introduction of Collett's 'Castles' in 1923. With hindsight it seems strange that the 'Castles' were built as a compromise because the Civil Engineer was not prepared to allow the proposed enlarged 'Star' design until many bridges had been strengthened. Thus came this 119-ton locomotive (with tender), which, with its 31,625 lbs. of tractive effort was claimed as the most powerful passenger engine in the country. No.4092 *Dunraven Castle,* coupled to a Churchward 'Intermediate' tender, stands with No.4078 *Pembroke Castle* on the pits at Old Oak Common, 15 August 1925. [L. T. George collection]

No.4086 *Builth Castle* at the head of the first part of the 'Cornish Riviera Limited' at Paddington, 29 August 1925. [P. J. T. Reed]

The Engine Testing Plant was installed at the eastern end of Swindon 'A' Shop when it was enlarged during 1901-03. Engines could be scientifically tested and the data obtained was used in the continuing development of Great Western motive power. It was not until the Nationalised era that the locomotives from other companies could be given such treatment (on the Rugby Testing Plant). 'Saint' No.2931 *Arlington Court* rests on the rollers, 2 June 1935; the framing has been raised to give free access to the steam chests, so possibly the valve events are to be studied. [L. T. George collection]

The 'A' Shop covered over 11 acres and usually the largest engines were constructed or repaired here. In its heyday, Swindon Works could build 100 and repair 1000 locomotives annually. The 4-6-0 under construction is No.5026 *Criccieth Castle,* so the date can be placed early in 1934. On the smokebox is chalked 'Lot 295' which was the order number for 'Castles' Nos.5023-32. Each batch of GW engines had its Lot Number, the final Lot under Great Western auspices before Nationalisation being No.366, which covered 'Modified Halls' Nos.6971-6990. [Peter Winding]

The Churchward Moguls had proved themselves invaluable to the operating authorities as they could tackle almost any reasonable task. Churchward had proposed a 4-6-0 to similar specifications, but in 1924, Collett rebuilt No.2925 *Saint Martin* with 6ft. diameter wheels for mixed-traffic duties. The rebuilt 4-6-0, then allocated to Penzance, had worked the 'Cornish Riviera' up through Cornwall to Plymouth (North Road) on Easter Saturday 11 April 1925. [P. J. T. Reed]

'Saint' No.2925 *Saint Martin* in post-Great War austerity guise—unlined paintwork and small diameter cast iron chimney. The engine is being prepared for an express duty at Landore, Swansea. It is to be hoped that the driver remembers that he has left the feeder by the buffer beam!

[Peter Winding collection]

The rebuilt 'Saint' proved so successful that a series of no less than eighty similar engines was ordered under Lot No.254 in 1927. The famous 'Halls' began to emerge from Swindon in 1928 and the initial order was completed in 1930. These magnificent engines continued in production until 1950 and were the inspiration of Stanier's 'Black Fives' and Thompson's 'B1s'. They were to be seen at work on all classes of traffic throughout the Great Western system's 'Red Routes' and played a prominent part in the West Country where their 6ft. wheels were ideal for the steep banks. No.4957 *Postlip Hall* speeds down the Cornish main line near Marazion in May 1940. [Brian A. Butt]

While modern engines of advanced design were rolling out of Swindon Works in increasing numbers, many interesting old stagers continued in service on the lesser duties. One engine which achieved particular fame was No.1473 of Armstrong's '517' Class 0-4-2T which acquired the name *Fair Rosamund* and was for many years employed on the Woodstock branch. The old engine has a full head of steam before heading out of Oxford with the branch train on 9 April 1927. [H. C. Casserley]

Although his mount weighs a mere 22 tons and boasts a tractive effort of only 5,194 lbs., the driver of 2-4-0T No.1300 nevertheless poses for the cameraman with as much pride as if he had charge of a mighty 'King'. The Victorian locomotive had originally been ordered for the South Devon Railway, having been designed, with its two sisters, as a broad gauge machine but the three were altered during construction to standard gauge. The scene is Hemyock on 25 May 1929. The final closure of this branch took place on 1 November 1975, when the milk processing plant at Hemyock ceased production. [H. C. Casserley]

Elderly Armstrong '517' Class 0-4-2T No.1436 in repose inside Swindon shed in June 1938. The 40-ton tank has 5ft. 2in. driving wheels and was one of 156 engines built between 1868 and 1885 for local passenger services. This example is fitted with a half-cab, an unpopular feature as little protection was given to the enginemen when running bunker-first. [L. T. George collection]

As with most of the early Great Western classes, detail differences could be discerned between individual members of the '517' class. For example, No.828, seen at Swindon, 6 July 1921, with its number displayed centrally on the side tank has a back to the cab and outside bearings to the trailing wheels. Note the driver's black box, an article favoured by most old time enginemen for carrying their personal belongings on the footplate. [L. T. George collection]

While the GW 'old-timers' were still hard at work on the secondary services, the powerful 'Kings' established themselves as the finest 4-6-0s in the country. With a tractive effort of over 40,000 lbs., they were the equal of the Pacifics of other companies and performed wonders on the heaviest express turns. Their 'Double Red' classification precluded their use on many routes and in Great Western days were usually to be seen on the Plymouth, Bristol and Wolverhampton turns only. The driver of No.6017 *King Edward IV* has shut off steam and coasts over the curves at Cowley Bridge Junction, near Exeter, with a *down* Plymouth express, while a Southern 'T9' waits for the road into Exeter with an *up* train from Plymouth, 26 August 1946.
[Brian A. Butt]

6017

'King' No.6028 *King Henry II* under repair in Swindon Works. This engine was renamed *King George VI* in 1937 upon the succession of that monarch. These large engines, built between 1927 and 1930, were the ultimate development of Churchward's four-cylinder concept and the Great Western was justly proud of its principal express design. The Standard No.12 boiler was pressed to 250 lbs. per sq. in., the highest figure then used by the GWR, while the tractive effort of 40,300 lbs. made the engines the most powerful passenger class in the country. [Peter Winding collection]

A 'King' at work on the road; No.6021 *King Richard II* heads a down Penzance express through Dawlish on 27 May 1939. The 'Kings' were particularly at home on the West of England expresses, and with their bigger boilers and larger firegrates had a reserve of power which gave them the edge over the 'Castles' when tackling the South Devon banks at the end of the 200-mile run from Paddington. [L. T. George collection]

The 'Kings' performed excellent work on the Birmingham 2-hour trains—in fact many commentators believed that these turns represented the finest locomotive work on the Great Western in the 1930s. Considering the performances recorded on such trains as the 'Riviera', 'Cheltenham Spa Express' and 'Bristolian', this was praise indeed. The turns were shared by Old Oak Common and Stafford Road (Wolverhampton) men. The Black Country shed had five 'Kings' in the late 1930s for its London turns. A 'King' is seen approaching the short tunnel at Brill on 22 June 1935. [H. C. Casserley]

Copper cap shining, safety valve bonnet polished, buffers and steam chests scoured, paintwork oiled over – this was the normal condition for a 'King' in the 1930s. Although the machinery of the GWR engines was so modern, they retained an air of Edwardian elegance which made them look old-fashioned alongside Stanier and Gresley machines on contemporary services. No.6004 *King George III* heads the up 'Cornish Riviera' around the Westbury Loop on 18 May 1936. [L. T. George collection]

Meanwhile, back with the veterans . . . a nicely-cleaned Deans Goods, No.2483, has pulled across to the up line at Dawlish in order to allow a down fast to come through. Many of these engines served in the two World Wars, and in the 1950s the design of the Dean blastpipe was adapted, successfully, in an effort to improve the steaming of the BR Standard Moguls. [Aubrey Parminter]

'Bulldogs' continued to work a number of the stopping trains between Bristol and Salisbury during the 1930s, the trains themselves usually running through to Portsmouth. The small GW shed at Salisbury normally had a couple of 'Bulldogs' among its half-dozen engines sub-shedded from Westbury during the 1930s. Salisbury Southern men also worked over this line to Bristol with passenger and excursion trains at this time. These two views show No.3364 *Frank Bibby* at Codford with ex-LSWR stock in tow on 5 July and 8 July 1938 respectively. [H. C. Casserley]

Curved-framed 'Bulldog' No.3308 *Falmouth* with express headlamps up works a Wolverhampton – Paddington train out of Stourbridge Junction. There was a strange fascination in the sight of the coupling rods whirling round outside the frames when these engines had worked up a good turn of speed.
[L. T. George collection]

A quiet time at Westbury shed on 23 May 1929. In the yard can be seen 'Bulldog' No.3384, Mogul No.6307 and 2-6-2T No.5536. The depot was opened in 1915, and in the 1930s had 60 or so engines on strength to cover a wide variety of duties, ranging from its Paddington top-link turns to the heavy freights to South Wales.
[H. C. Casserley]

No.3449 *Nightingale* assists No.5016 *Montgomery Castle* on the heavy summer Saturday 11.0a.m. Paddington – Penzance, 8 August 1936. The train has stopped at Par, in Cornwall, to set down the Newquay passengers.

[P. J. T. Reed]

Eight-coupled power for a South Devon 'stopper' in the 1930s. Churchward mixed-traffic 2-8-0 No.4706 pulls away from the waterside station at Dawlish with a local to Exeter, probably a filling-in turn between its normal duties on heavy night fitted freights. [Aubrey Parminter]

The driver peers ahead from the footplate of an unidentified '28xx' as a heavy freight makes its cautious descent down Dainton Bank on 23 September 1946. These 2-8-0s were straightforward and unpretentious work-horses and were ideal for such slogging freight turns. [Brian A. Butt]

Eight-coupled wheels again, this time providing the motive power for a down freight at Stourbridge Junction, shortly after Grouping. This Churchward 4ft. 7½in. 2-8-0 No.2818 has been preserved and is now the property of Bristol City Museum. [L. T. George collection]

The famous '45s' were developed from the '44xx' 2-6-2Ts of 1904. These spritely 55-tonners had smaller wheels at 4ft. 1½ins. and in their early years were mainly concentrated in the West Country. No.4403, seen at St. Erth on 9 August 1923, was the St. Ives branch engine at that time.

[P. J. T. Reed]

One of Churchward's most successful designs was his small 2-6-2 tank, the '45xx' Class. These 57-ton engines, with 4ft. 7½in. wheels, were the ideal power for the Company's branch lines, especially those with steep gradients, as they had remarkable powers of acceleration. No.5535, one of the later '4575' series with the larger sloping side tanks, hurries a Witham-Yatton local away from Cheddar, 7 May 1936. [L. T. George collection]

Although a large number of 'Halls' were in service by the mid-1930s, there was still plenty of top-class work for the Moguls to perform. No.6387, built by Robert Stephenson Ltd. in 1921, carries express headlights as it pounds along the main line near Castle Cary with an up Weymouth on 24 April 1936. Notching-up was not easy with the heavy lever-reverse when these engines were travelling at speed, while the riding could be quite lively, to put it mildly, when they were really given their head. [L. T. George collection]

No.4054 *Princess Charlotte* at Torquay with an express train in the 1930s. The driver snatches an uncomfortable rest sitting on the cab cut-out while waiting for the road! [Peter Winding]

'Star' Class No.4049 *Princess Maud* near Box with a running-in turn, a local Bristol to Swindon passenger on 22 June 1936, after a visit to Swindon for a heavy general and repaint. The engine has been fitted with outside steam pipes and a high-sided tender, but retains the tall safety valve bonnet, a combination which particularly suited these grand ladies. [L. T. George collection]

A Penzance – Liverpool express rolls around the curves along the sea wall at Dawlish on 3 June 1939 behind 'Star' No.4017 *Knight of Liége.* By the late 1930s, the majority of 'Stars' were shedded away from the West of England, although Newton Abbot retained No.4012 until the post-war years. Bath Road, Bristol, had the largest allocation, twelve in number, in 1938.
[L. T. George collection]

49

Even the powerful 'Kings' required assistance over the South Devon banks if their load exceeded 360 tons, so the use of pilot engines was a feature of the operation of this main line. Newton Abbot and Laira used whatever engines were available during periods of intense traffic, and it was one of Britain's greatest railway events to see, and hear, a heavy train storming the mountainous grades with two 4-6-0s at the head. On 28 September 1946, No.4991 *Cobham Hall* was pilot to a 'King' on the gruelling climb up to Dainton Tunnel. The fireman on the 'King' has filled the box to capacity, shut the firebox door, turned on the injector and has then left the engine to to do its stuff. Judging by the plume of steam from the safety valves she is responding magnificently.
[Brian A. Butt]

Collett introduced the '2251' 0-6-0 in 1930 to replace the ageing 'Dean Goods' and Cambrian 0-6-0s. The machinery was similar to the Dean design, but a modern boiler was mounted on the chassis, which, with the Collett side-window cab, gave the engine an up-to-date appearance. The class eventually numbered 120 members, and having the classification 'Yellow C' was able to work on the majority of the Company's routes. Although Taunton had a sizeable allocation for the Minehead services, they were rarely seen in the far west, but they could be found almost everywhere else, working light freight and passenger trains. Their 5ft. 2in. wheels made them ideal light mixed traffic units. No.2254 is seen at Cheltenham.

[L. T. George collection]

Another Collett lightweight class was the '32xx' 4-4-0 introduced in 1936. These interesting engines were a hybrid design, incorporating a 'Duke' boiler on 'Bulldog' frames, and were originally named 'Earls'. They were mainly to be found in Wales, on the ex-Cambrian lines which had a light axle-loading limit. The 5ft. 8in. wheels and 180 lb. per sq. in. boiler gave these little engines a tractive effort of 18,955 lbs., and although of Victorian appearance, they continued in service until the final years of steam working. No.3211 is on shed at Oswestry, 25 September 1938. [L. T. George collection]

Although the 4-6-0's stole most of the Great Western limelight, the humble 0-6-0 pannier tanks still formed a very large proportion of the total locomotive stock, and much of the work was performed by the various varieties of these engines. The Collett '57xxs' were introduced in 1929, being a more powerful version of Dean's '2721' Class of 1897. The saturated boiler was pressed to 200 lb. per sq. in., and with their 4ft. 7½in. wheels these tanks performed on a wide range of duties, from shunting, through light goods work, to branch passenger trains. No.5760 is seen working a short down goods along the coastal line near Dawlish on 21 July 1936. [L. T. George collection]

Collett modified his panniers slightly in 1933, the main changes being in the cab, which had a new roof profile and larger windows. In all a grand total of 863 engines of the '57xx' Class were built, a tribute to their usefulness – in fact, it has been said of the Great Western that it *could* have been run with 'Halls' and '57s', an exaggeration of course, but yet containing a modicum of truth. No.9732, built January 1935, ambles through pastoral scenery near Shepton Mallet with a Cranmore to Yatton goods on 17 March 1936. [L. T. George collection]

During the worst years of the Depression in the early 1930s, there was a considerable decrease in Welsh coal traffic and as a consequence, many of the splendid '42xx' 2-8-0Ts were standing idle. In 1934 the first of the '72xx' tanks appeared, being a 2-8-2T rebuild of the original 2-8-0T No.5275. The coal capacity was increased to 6 tons and the tank capacity became 2,500 gallons. With this fuel supply, a '72' could range far and wide around the Railway with heavy freight trains and in all 54 engines were converted between 1934 and 1939. No.7204 (ex No.5279) works on up goods near Churchdown on 25 July 1939. At that date all but five of the class were shedded in South Wales, four being at Banbury and one at Oxley.
[L. T. George collection]

A '43xx' 2-6-0 at Aller Junction, near Newton Abbot, with a goods in the early 1930s.
[Aubrey Parminter]

Churchward's final '28', No.2883 was built in 1919. In March 1938 No.2884 emerged from Swindon, being mechanically similar to her earlier sisters, but having such modern features as outside steam pipes, side-window cab and short safety-valve bonnet. The new engines took their places alongside the old '28s' in the same links and the 84 new machines proved invaluable during the war years when there was a tremendous increase of freight traffic on the GWR. No.2894 at Swindon, 26 March 1939.
[L. T. George collection]

Churchward's original concept of a 5ft. 8in. 4-6-0 came into being with the appearance of the 'Granges' in 1936. The question as to why they were built has often been asked, as they virtually duplicated the 'Halls', but in fact, they were classified as rebuilds of '43xx' 2-6-0s and as such were not accounted as capital expenditure. In truth, little more than the wheels of the withdrawn Moguls were used in the 'rebuilds', which proved to be popular performers on the steep gradients of the West of England main lines. No.6838 *Goodmoor Grange* works a down express through Dawlish shortly after it was built in 1937.

[L. T. George collection]

Collett's final design of 4-6-0 was the small '78xx' 'Manor' Class which appeared in 1938. Again nominally rebuilds of withdrawn '43xx' Moguls, the '78s' were a lightweight version of the 'Granges', the main difference being their Standard No.14 boiler which was smaller than the Standard No.1 fitted to the 'Halls', 'Granges', 'Saints' and 'Stars'. The 'Manors' were Blue Route engines and so were seen where no 4-6-0 had ever run before, for example on the Cambrian lines and Cheltenham – Andover Junction. No.7810 *'Draycott Manor',* seen near Churchdown, was working the Newcastle – Swansea express on 25 July 1939, the service on which they made their initial appearance. [L. T. George collection]

Pannier tanks, ancient and modern, at Swindon Works on 4 April 1946. No.2060, of the '2021' Class of 4ft. 1½in. 0-6-0PTs and No.6417, one of the 1932-built '64xx' 4ft. 7½in. 0-6-0PTs have both been smartened up with a repaint after the years of war-time neglect. [H. C. Casserley]

A picturesque line-up of elderly engines inside the shed at Swindon, 27 September 1936. This large depot had two turntable units and a nine-road straight shed under its vast roof, and at the close of the GWR's existence in 1947 had 118 engines on its strength. These included a pair of 'Castles', half a dozen 'Stars' and a wide range of smaller engines. [L. T. George collection]

The '32s' were usually called 'Dukedogs', a reference to their mixed ancestry. Nos.3210 and 3213 stand outside the old shed at Aberystwyth, which was demolished in 1938 and replaced with a new building. There were usually half-a-dozen '32xxs' sub-shedded here from Machynlleth for working the shed's passenger turns. [Peter Winding collection]

'Duke' 4-4-0 No.3256 *Guinevere* reposes in the Stock Shed at Swindon, the depot where spare engines could be stored. These 4-4-0s, introduced in 1895 were graceful Victorian ladies, the curved double frames and enormous domes imparting a sense of something 'different' amongst the vast army of domeless standard passenger engines. Eleven of these old stalwarts remained in service at Nationalisation, mainly working in Central Wales, although Didcot, Shrewsbury and Stourbridge Junction had representatives.
[Peter Winding]

25-ton 0-4-0ST No.92 inside the shed at Stafford Road, Wolverhampton. This little engine was built by Beyer, Peacock (No.51) in 1857 as an 0-4-2ST, being rebuilt as an 0-4-0ST at Chester in 1878. Further modernisation took place at the end of the century and she remained in service until 1942. [Peter Winding collection]

No.96, built by Sharp Stewart in 1856 for the Birkenhead Railway, was rebuilt at Wolverhampton Works in 1890, and as such bore a resemblance to No.92. This little machine was withdrawn in 1935. [Peter Winding collection]

A series of 85 'Castles' emerged from Swindon between 1932 and 1939, when production of express engines ceased with the outbreak of war. Many of these locomotives received changes of name and a large proportion had names other than castles. No.5069 came out of the Works as *Isambard Kingdom Brunel* in June 1938 with the name mounted on a large radius nameplate, which looked most peculiar on this otherwise graceful 4-6-0. However, the great engineer was commemorated in this unsightly way for a short while only and in July, new plates of standard radius were fitted, and these were among the most impressive of all GWR plates. [L. T. George collection]

Surely the definitive photograph of a Great Western express train of the 1930s! A polished 'Castle' (No.5035 *Coity Castle*) and immaculate chocolate-and-cream coaching stock set against the sun-drenched South Devon beaches near Dawlish – this was the image which the vigorous publicity department of the Company put across at every opportunity. The GWR built up a tremendous reputation in the West of England and in spite of the speedy diesel-hauled services running today there are many older inhabitants of the region who still recall the old Company with real affection.
[L. T. George collection]

'Castle' No.5079 *Lysander* was one of five of the class converted to oil-burning in the post-war years, running in this condition from January 1947 to October 1948. This 'Castle' was allocated to Laira shed and usually worked the 9.15 a.m. Plymouth to Penzance, returning home with the heavy 1.25 p.m. from Penzance. The oil-burners had the fuel tanks mounted on the top of the tenders and were provided with sliding shutters on the cab-sides. With skilled crews these engines steamed well and it was unfortunate that this Great Western experiment, which preceded the official government-sponsored scheme, was terminated for economic and political reasons soon after Nationalisation.
[Brian A. Butt]

5079

The Great Western liked to be 'with it' (to use a later idiom!) and so in March 1935, a 'King' and 'Castle' were treated to 'semi-streamlining', with strange cowls and fairing adorning the locomotives. The results were universally unpopular with railwaymen (because of the added restrictions to the 'works' of the engines) and to enthusiasts alike. Various bits and pieces began to disappear almost immediately until eventually No.5005 *Manorbier Castle* returned to normal, but No.6014 *King Henry VII* retained the wedge-shaped cab until withdrawal in 1962. The latter engine is seen on the turntable at Kingswear on 25 November 1935. [L. T. George collection]

How a 'King' *should* look. No.6016 *King Edward V* has a full head of steam as it hauls a down express away from Aller Junction on 28 September 1946. The post-war Hawksworth livery looked excellent on these big 4-6-0s.
[Brian A. Butt]

No.4099 *Kilgerran Castle* waits for departure time at Exeter (St. Davids) with a local train for Plymouth.
[Brian A. Butt]

The Hawksworth 'Counties' were the last of the long and illustrious line of Great Western express engines. A development of the 'Modified Halls' of 1944, these 125-ton two-cylinder engines appeared in August 1945, just in time for the peace! Although possessing certain features new to the GWR, such as the double chimney on No.1000 and 6ft. 3in. driving wheels, a 280 lbs. per sq. in. boiler, continuous splashers and a flat-sided tender, they were nevertheless still completely recognisable as descendants of the early Churchward 4-6-0s.A number of the class were stationed in Cornwall; No.1022 *County of Northampton* takes water at Truro in 1947. The tenders (numbered 100-129), holding 7 tons of coal and 4,000 gallons of water, were only used with the 'Counties' as they were wider than the standard tenders and matched the full-width cabs of these 4-6-0s. [Brian A. Butt]

Having been designed during the wars years, when express locomotives were not allowed to be developed, the 'Counties', with their 6ft. 3in. wheels were officially mixed-traffics, although they performed the majority of their miles on passenger turns. However, No.1001 *County of Bucks* has a turn up the Cornish main line, and is seen near Gwinear Road, with a train of cattle wagons, which are probably loaded with potatoes, as during the early summer of 1947, a procession of potato specials ran from Cornwall to London to relieve the shortage of food in the capital. The two 18½in. x 30in. cylinders developed considerable power (32,580 lbs. of tractive effort) and the engines imparted considerable surging to the leading vehicles of their trains when accelerating repidly from rest. [Brian A. Butt]

G W R

A final look at a pair of tried and trusted old-timers. Churchward '45xx' 2-6-2T No.4569 blows off at 180 lbs. per sq. in. while waiting at Falmouth. Behind the buffer beam can be seen the letters TR, the code for its home shed of Truro. Each depot had an easily-identifiable letter code, which was much easier to interpret than the British Railways LMS-inspired system. However, the latest diesel depot codes are reminiscent of the old GW system. [Peter Winding]

First introduced as saddle tanks by Armstrong in 1874, the '1901' Class were rebuilt as panniers in the early years of the century. With 4ft. 1½in. wheels and a tractive effort of 17,410 lbs., these old engines performed as light shunters and station pilots for many more years. Forty-three saw Nationalisation and the last example was withdrawn in 1959; No.1967 shunts at Burry Port on 7 July 1947. [H. C. Casserley]

The Great Western used auto-cars on many of its light branch services, often worked by the diminutive '48xx' 0-4-2Ts (which were later renumbered in the '14xx' series). One of these tanks propels the auto-car out from Buckfastleigh on the last lap of its trip to Ashburton on 28 September 1946. Fortunately, such a scene has not entirely gone for ever from the West Country, as the Dart Valley Railway now operates this line between Totnes and Buckfastleigh with similar equipment. [Brian A. Butt]

Postscript – where it all happened, the Locomotive Offices at Swindon Works. The stone engravings serve as a reminder of the great days of the broad gauge, and inside, the wonderful range of locomotives, sired by Churchward, was planned and drawn by the C.M.E's staff. [H. C. Casserley]